# Make Every Day Special

# *Making It Special*

Yes, *PHILADELPHIA BRAND Cream Cheese can help you make every day special. This all-new collection of quick-to-fix recipes developed by the Kraft Creative Kitchens will help transform everyday events—from casual family suppers, to spontaneous gatherings of friends, to elegant dinner parties—into memorable occasions. Read on for helpful tips on how to ensure recipe success with each of your culinary creations.*

*For starters, who said delicious cheesecakes can't be simple? Try this luscious PHILLY 3-STEP™ Cheesecake tonight!*

## PHILLY 3-STEP™ CHEESECAKE

**Prep time: 10 minutes**
**Cook time: 40 minutes**

1.

**1. MIX** 2 pkgs. (8 oz. each) PHILADELPHIA BRAND Cream Cheese, softened, ½ cup sugar and ½ teaspoon vanilla at medium speed with electric mixer until well blended. Add 2 eggs; mix until blended.

**2. POUR** into KEEBLER® READY CRUST™ Graham Cracker Pie Crust (6 oz. *or* 9 inch).

2.

**3. BAKE** at 350°F, 40 minutes or until center is almost set. Cool. Refrigerate 3 hours or overnight.
*Makes 8 servings*

3.

# CHEESECAKE TIPS FROM THE KRAFT CREATIVE KITCHENS

**To prevent cracking, follow these quick mixing and baking hints:**

## Mixing

- *Soften PHILLY Cream Cheese before mixing.* To soften in microwave: place one completely unwrapped (8 oz.) package in microwavable bowl. Microwave on HIGH 15 seconds. Add 15 seconds for each additional package of PHILLY Cream Cheese.

- *Don't overbeat.* Beat at low speed after adding eggs, just until blended. Gently stir in any flavoring ingredients (chocolate chips, fruit, etc.) at the very end of mixing.

## Baking and Cooling

- *Bake in a moist oven.* When preheating oven, place a 13×9-inch baking pan half filled with hot tap water on bottom rack of oven. Bake cheesecake on middle rack above pan of water.

- *Don't peek* into oven during baking.

- *Don't overbake.* When done, edges should be slightly puffed. The center area, about the size of a silver dollar, should still appear soft and moist. The center will firm upon cooling.

- *Cool cheesecake on wire rack* at room temperature for 1 hour before refrigerating.

## Freezing

- Prepare cheesecake as directed, omitting topping. Wrap securely in plastic wrap; overwrap with foil. Place in plastic bag; label, date and seal. Freeze up to 2 months.

- Thaw wrapped cheesecake in refrigerator overnight.

You may substitute PHILLY Neufchâtel Cheese, ⅓ Less Fat than Cream Cheese, for cream cheese in any of these recipes.

# SPRINGFORM PAN CHEESECAKES

***Easy steps toward success:***

## *Crust*

For baked springform pan cheesecakes, prepare crust by pressing crust mixture into pan. A mixture of graham cracker crumbs, sugar and melted butter or margarine is shown here.

## *Loosening Cheesecake from Pan*

Immediately upon removal from oven, run a thin metal spatula or knife around edge of cheesecake (pushing against side of pan) to loosen it from side of pan. Keep spring fastener on side of pan locked and springform pan side on. Cool 1 hour at room temperature; refrigerate.

## *Removing Pan*

Loosen spring fastener. Lift rim of pan straight up to separate it from cheesecake.

# CHEESECAKE CREATIVE CRUSTS

**Whether you are making a classic cheesecake in a springform pan or a PHILLY 3-STEP™ Cheesecake, these creative crusts are sure to be hits.**

## Graham Cracker Crust

Mix 1½ cups graham cracker crumbs, 3 tablespoons sugar and ¼ cup butter or margarine, melted. Press onto bottom and sides of 9-inch pie plate or bottom of springform pan. Pour cheesecake batter into unbaked crust.

## Spiced Graham Cracker Crust

Add ½ teaspoon ground cinnamon or ¼ teaspoon ground ginger.

## Nut Crust

Substitute ½ cup firmly chopped pecans, almonds, walnuts, peanuts or macadamia nuts for ½ cup of the graham cracker crumbs.

## Chocolate Cookie Crust

Omit sugar and reduce butter or margarine to 2 tablespoons. Substitute finely crushed chocolate sandwich cookies for graham cracker crumbs.

# QUICK TOPPINGS

**Before serving, top your favorite cheesecake with one of these easy toppings.**

- Drizzle caramel or chocolate ice cream topping over cheesecake.
- Spread BREAKSTONE'S or KNUDSEN Sour Cream or COOL WHIP Whipped Topping over cheesecake; top with fresh fruit slices.
- Spoon canned pie filling over cheesecake.
- For a beautiful design, place a paper doily or cut paper pattern on top of cheesecake. Sprinkle generously with powdered sugar or unsweetened cocoa. Carefully lift doily with a straight upward motion.

# GREAT GARNISHES

**Try these finishing touches to make your recipes extra special.**

## Fresh Herbs

Look for fresh herbs in the produce section of your supermarket. In addition to parsley, a sprig of fresh basil, oregano, thyme or rosemary can add an elegant touch to even the most simple savory dish.

## Cucumber Ribbons

Cut thin lengthwise strips around cucumber with vegetable peeler, making sure there is a line of green peel on both sides of each strip. Place strips in ice water to chill; drain well. Gently gather cucumber strips to form decorative ruffles.

## Citrus Fruit Twists

Cut 1 lemon, lime or orange into slices. Discard slices toward ends. Make small cut in middle of each slice from center down through peel. Twist slices into spirals.

## Chocolate Drizzle

Place 1 square BAKER'S Semi-Sweet Chocolate in plastic zippered sandwich bag. Close bag tightly. Microwave on HIGH 1 minute or until chocolate is melted. Fold down top of bag tightly; snip tiny piece off 1 corner. Holding bag tightly, drizzle chocolate through opening.

## Dipping Fruit and Nuts

Melt BAKER'S Semi-Sweet Chocolate. Dip fruit or nuts into melted chocolate, covering at least half; let excess chocolate drip off. Arrange on wax paper-lined tray. Refrigerate until chocolate is firm. Do not freeze.

# DIP TIPS FROM THE KRAFT CREATIVE KITCHENS

## PHILLY® Quick Spreads

- Open a package of PHILLY Cream Cheese and top it with your choice of toppings—salsa, pesto sauce, orange marmalade or hot pepper jelly—the possibilities are endless. Or, for a different presentation, spread cream cheese on a serving platter and top with your favorite topping.

- To make a simple holiday appetizer, cut one package PHILLY in half diagonally. Place triangles together to form Christmas tree. Top with salsa and green pepper strips. Use a cinnamon stick for "trunk."

## PHILLY® Quick Dips

- Soften PHILLY Cream Cheese before mixing (page 3).

- For best results, first beat PHILLY Cream Cheese and milk together in electric mixer until well blended. Then, stir in remaining ingredients.

- Making dips and storing in refrigerator a day ahead of time allows flavors to blend. Stir before serving.

- To enhance flavor, remove dips from refrigerator 15 minutes before serving.

## Dipper Tips

- Cut up vegetable dippers ahead of time; cover with damp paper towel and store in resealable plastic bags in the refrigerator.

- Zucchini, green beans, pea pods and jicama are interesting and delicious additions to a traditional vegetable dipper tray.

- Cut out colorful red, green, yellow and orange bell peppers or other vegetables with small canapé or cookie cutters for interesting shapes, such as tiny stars or leaves for vegetable platters.

- Dip fresh fruit slices, such as apples, pears and bananas, in lemon juice to prevent browning.

- Use hollowed out red, green or yellow bell pepper as colorful bowl to hold your PHILLY dip.

# _Easy Dips & Spreads_

## PHILLY® Garlic & Herb Dip

*Prep time: 10 minutes plus refrigerating*

**1 pkg. (8 oz.) PHILADELPHIA BRAND Cream
    Cheese, softened**
**3 Tbsp. milk**
**3 Tbsp. finely chopped fresh basil**
**3 Tbsp. finely chopped fresh parsley**
**2 Tbsp. chopped fresh chives**
**1 clove garlic, minced**

**MIX** cream cheese and milk with electric mixer on medium speed
until smooth.

**BLEND** in remaining ingredients. Refrigerate. Serve with assorted
cut-up vegetables, breadsticks or chips. Garnish, if desired.

*Makes 1 cup*

**PHILLY® Garlic & Herb Dip**

# PHILLY® Salsa Dip

**Prep time:** *5 minutes plus refrigerating*

**1 pkg. (8 oz.) PHILADELPHIA BRAND Cream Cheese, softened**
**½ cup salsa**

**BEAT** cream cheese with electric mixer on medium speed until smooth.

**BLEND** in salsa. Refrigerate. Serve with tortilla chips or assorted cut-up vegetables. Garnish, if desired. *Makes 1½ cups*

**Simple Salsa Appetizer:** *Place cream cheese on serving plate; top with salsa.*

**PHILLY® Salsa Dip**

# PHILLY® Cranberry Orange Spread

*Prep time: 5 minutes*

**1 pkg. (8 oz.) PHILADELPHIA BRAND Cream
Cheese, softened
½ cup cranberry orange sauce
3 Tbsp. chopped pecans, toasted**

**PLACE** cream cheese on serving plate.

**TOP** with sauce; sprinkle with pecans. Serve with crackers.
Garnish, if desired.                                    *Makes 10 servings*

# Hot Crab Dip

*Prep time: 10 minutes    Baking time: 30 minutes*

**2 pkg. (8 oz. each) PHILADELPHIA BRAND
Cream Cheese, softened
2 cans (6 oz. each) crabmeat, drained, flaked
½ cup (2 oz.) KRAFT Shredded Parmesan
Cheese
¼ cup chopped green onions
2 Tbsp. white wine
2 tsp. KRAFT Prepared Horseradish
¼ tsp. hot pepper sauce**

**MIX** all ingredients with electric mixer on medium speed until
well blended.

**SPOON** into 9-inch pie plate or quiche dish.

**BAKE** at 350°F for 25 to 30 minutes or until lightly browned.
Serve with crackers.                              *Makes 10 to 12 servings*

# PHILLY® Greek-Style Spread

*Prep time: 10 minutes*

**1 pkg. (8 oz.) PHILADELPHIA BRAND Cream
    Cheese, softened**
**½ cup chopped tomato**
**¼ cup chopped pitted niçoise olives**
**¼ cup finely chopped cucumber**
**1 tsp. olive oil**
**½ tsp. dried oregano leaves, crushed**

*SPREAD* cream cheese on serving plate.

*MIX* remaining ingredients; spoon over cream cheese. Serve with crackers or toasted pita bread wedges.            *Makes 10 servings*

# Mediterranean Dip

*Prep time: 10 minutes plus refrigerating*

**1 pkg. (8 oz.) PHILADELPHIA BRAND Cream
    Cheese, softened**
**2 Tbsp. milk**
**2 tsp. red wine vinegar**
**1 clove garlic, minced**
**1 tsp. lemon and pepper seasoning salt**
**½ tsp. dried oregano leaves, crushed**

*MIX* cream cheese, milk and vinegar with electric mixer on medium speed until smooth.

*BLEND* in remaining ingredients. Refrigerate. Serve with lavosh crackers or toasted pita bread wedges (page 28).            *Makes 1 cup*

# PHILLY® Pesto Dip

*Prep time: 5 minutes plus refrigerating*

**1 pkg. (8 oz.) PHILADELPHIA BRAND Cream
     Cheese, softened
3 Tbsp. milk
⅓ cup DI GIORNO Pesto Sauce**

*MIX* cream cheese and milk with electric mixer on medium speed until smooth.

*BLEND* in pesto sauce. Refrigerate. Serve with assorted cut-up vegetables, breadsticks or chips.                     *Makes 1½ cups*

# PHILLY® Crabmeat Spread

*Prep time: 5 minutes*

**1 pkg. (8 oz.) PHILADELPHIA BRAND Cream
     Cheese, softened
¼ cup cocktail sauce
1 pkg. (8 oz.) imitation crabmeat *or* 1 pkg.
     (6 oz.) frozen cooked tiny shrimp, thawed,
     drained**

*SPREAD* cream cheese on serving plate.

*POUR* cocktail sauce over cream cheese; top with imitation crabmeat. Serve with crackers or cocktail rye bread slices.
                                                           *Makes 10 servings*

# Chili Cheese Dip

*Prep time:* 5 minutes    *Baking time:* 25 minutes

**1 pkg. (8 oz.) PHILADELPHIA BRAND Cream
    Cheese, softened
1 can (15 oz.) chili
1 cup (4 oz.) KRAFT Natural Shredded Sharp
    Cheddar Cheese**

*SPREAD* cream cheese on bottom of 9-inch pie plate or quiche dish. Spread with chili; sprinkle with cheddar cheese.

*BAKE* at 350°F for 20 to 25 minutes or until cheese is melted. Serve with tortilla chips. Garnish, if desired.

*Makes 8 to 10 servings*

# PHILLY® Hot Pepper Spread

*Prep time:* 5 minutes

**1 pkg. (8 oz.) PHILADELPHIA BRAND Cream
    Cheese, softened
¼ cup hot pepper jelly
2 Tbsp. chopped green onion**

*PLACE* cream cheese on serving plate.

*TOP* with jelly; sprinkle with onion. Serve with crackers.

*Makes 10 servings*

*Chili Cheese Dip*

# PHILLY® Refreshing Dill Dip

*Prep time: 10 minutes plus refrigerating*

**1 pkg. (8 oz.) PHILADELPHIA BRAND Cream
   Cheese, softened**
**½ cup KRAFT Ranch Dressing**
**2 Tbsp. milk**
**1 medium cucumber, peeled, seeded, chopped**
**2 Tbsp. finely chopped onion**
**1½ tsp. dill weed**

**MIX** cream cheese, dressing and milk with electric mixer on medium speed until smooth.

**BLEND** in remaining ingredients. Refrigerate. Serve with assorted cut-up vegetables. Garnish, if desired.          *Makes 3 cups*

# Roasted Red Pepper Dip

*Prep time: 10 minutes plus refrigerating*

**1 pkg. (8 oz.) PHILADELPHIA BRAND Cream
   Cheese, softened**
**3 Tbsp. milk**
**½ cup chopped drained roasted red peppers**
**½ tsp. dried thyme leaves**
**⅛ tsp. ground black pepper**

**MIX** cream cheese and milk with electric mixer on medium speed until smooth.

**BLEND** in remaining ingredients. Refrigerate. Serve with assorted cut-up vegetables, breadsticks or chips.          *Makes 1¾ cups*

*PHILLY® Refreshing Dill Dip*

# Spinach Dip

*Prep time: 10 minutes plus refrigerating*

**1 pkg. (8 oz.) PHILADELPHIA BRAND Cream
    Cheese, softened**
**¼ cup milk**
**1 pkg. (10 oz.) frozen chopped spinach,
    thawed, drained**
**1 can (8 oz.) water chestnuts, drained,
    chopped**
**½ cup chopped red pepper**
**½ tsp. garlic salt**
**⅛ tsp. hot pepper sauce**

*MIX* cream cheese and milk with electric mixer on medium speed
until smooth.

*BLEND* in remaining ingredients. Refrigerate. Serve with assorted
cut-up vegetables or chips.                    *Makes 3 cups*

*Spinach Dip*

# Cheesecake Creme Dip

*Prep time: 5 minutes plus refrigerating*

**1 pkg. (8 oz.) PHILADELPHIA BRAND Cream
    Cheese, softened
1 jar (7 oz.) marshmallow creme**

***MIX*** cream cheese and marshmallow creme with electric mixer on medium speed until well blended. Refrigerate.

***SERVE*** with assorted cut-up fresh fruit or pound cake cubes. Garnish, if desired. *Makes 1³/₄ cups*

# PHILLY® Fruit Dip

*Prep time: 5 minutes plus refrigerating*

**1 pkg. (8 oz.) PHILADELPHIA BRAND Cream
    Cheese, softened
1 container (8 oz.) strawberry *or* any flavored
    yogurt**

***MIX*** cream cheese and yogurt with electric mixer on medium speed until well blended. Refrigerate.

***SERVE*** with assorted fresh fruit. *Makes about 1²/₃ cups*

*Cheesecake Creme Dip*

*Elegant Appetizers*

## Roasted Red Pepper Pesto Cheesecake

*Prep time: 15 minutes    Baking time: 1 hour*

> 1 cup butter-flavored cracker crumbs (about 40 crackers)
> ¼ cup (½ stick) butter *or* margarine
> 2 pkg. (8 oz. each) PHILADELPHIA BRAND Cream Cheese, softened
> 1 cup ricotta cheese
> 3 eggs
> ½ cup (2 oz.) KRAFT 100% Grated Parmesan Cheese
> ½ cup DI GIORNO Pesto Sauce
> ½ cup drained roasted red peppers, puréed

**MIX** crumbs and butter. Press onto bottom of 9-inch springform pan. Bake at 325°F for 10 minutes.

**MIX** cream cheese and ricotta cheese with electric mixer on medium speed until well blended. Add eggs, 1 at a time, mixing well after each addition. Blend in remaining ingredients. Pour over crust.

**BAKE** at 325°F for 55 minutes to 1 hour. Run knife or metal spatula around rim of pan to loosen cake; cool before removing rim of pan. Refrigerate 4 hours or overnight. Let stand 15 minutes at room temperature before serving. Garnish, if desired. Serve with crackers.                                    *Makes 12 to 14 servings*

*Also great served with fresh fruit for brunch.*

**Roasted Red Pepper
Pesto Cheesecake**

# Savory Bruschetta

**Prep time:** *15 minutes*    **Baking time:** *10 minutes*

- ¼ **cup olive oil**
- 1 **clove garlic, minced**
- 1 **loaf (1 lb.) French bread, cut in half lengthwise**
- 1 **pkg. (8 oz.) PHILADELPHIA BRAND Cream Cheese, softened**
- 3 **Tbsp. KRAFT 100% Grated Parmesan Cheese**
- 2 **Tbsp. chopped pitted niçoise olives**
- 1 **cup chopped plum tomatoes**
  **Fresh basil leaves**

*MIX* oil and garlic; spread on cut surfaces of bread. Bake at 400°F for 8 to 10 minutes or until toasted. Cool.

*MIX* cream cheese and Parmesan cheese with electric mixer on medium speed until blended. Stir in olives. Spread on cooled bread halves.

*TOP* with tomatoes and basil leaves. Cut diagonally into slices.

*Makes 2 dozen*

*Savory Bruschetta*

# Hot Artichoke Dip

*Prep time: 15 minutes    Baking time: 25 minutes*

**1 pkg. (8 oz.) PHILADELPHIA BRAND Cream
Cheese, softened**
**1 can (14 oz.) artichoke hearts, drained,
chopped**
**½ cup KRAFT Real Mayonnaise**
**½ cup (2 oz.) KRAFT 100% Grated Parmesan
Cheese**
**2 Tbsp. finely chopped fresh basil *or* 1 tsp.
dried basil leaves**
**2 Tbsp. finely chopped red onion**
**1 clove garlic, minced**
**½ cup chopped tomato**

*MIX* cream cheese and all remaining ingredients except tomato
with electric mixer on medium speed until well blended.

*SPOON* into 9-inch quiche dish or pie plate.

*BAKE* at 350°F for 25 minutes. Sprinkle with tomato. Serve with
assorted cut-up vegetables or toasted pita bread wedges. Garnish, if
desired.                                               *Makes 3¼ cups*

**To make toasted pita bread wedges,** cut 3 split pita breads each
into 8 triangles. Place on cookie sheet. Bake at 350°F for 10 to
12 minutes or until crisp.

*Hot Artichoke Dip*

# Spinach Cheese Triangles

*Prep time: 30 minutes*    *Baking time: 15 minutes*

**1 pkg. (8 oz.) PHILADELPHIA BRAND Cream
    Cheese, softened**
**1 pkg. (10 oz.) frozen chopped spinach,
    thawed, well drained**
**⅓ cup chopped drained roasted red peppers**
**¼ tsp. garlic salt**
**6 sheets frozen phyllo, thawed**
**½ cup (1 stick) butter or margarine, melted**

*MIX* cream cheese, spinach, red peppers and garlic salt with electric mixer on medium speed until well blended.

*LAY* 1 phyllo sheet on flat surface. Brush with some of the melted butter. Cut lengthwise into 4 (18×3½-inch) strips.

*SPOON* about 1 Tbsp. filling about 1 inch from one end of each strip. Fold the end over the filling at a 45-degree angle. Continue folding as you would fold a flag to form a triangle that encloses filling. Repeat procedure with remaining phyllo sheets. Place triangles on cookie sheet. Brush with melted butter.

*BAKE* at 375°F for 12 to 15 minutes or until golden brown.

*Makes 3 dozen*

**Tip:** Unfold phyllo sheets; cover with wax paper and damp towel to prevent drying until ready to use.

# Cheese and Nut Roll

*Prep time: 20 minutes plus refrigerating*

**1½ cups (6 oz.) KRAFT Natural Shredded Sharp
    Cheddar Cheese
1 pkg. (8 oz.) PHILADELPHIA BRAND Cream
    Cheese, softened, divided
2 Tbsp. finely chopped green onion
2 Tbsp. finely chopped red pepper
1 small clove garlic, minced
½ cup (2 oz.) KRAFT Blue Cheese Crumbles
2 Tbsp. milk
½ cup finely chopped pistachio nuts**

*MIX* cheddar cheese and ½ of the cream cheese with electric mixer on medium speed until well blended. Add onion, red pepper and garlic; mix well. Refrigerate 30 minutes.

*MIX* remaining cream cheese, blue cheese and milk with electric mixer on medium speed until well blended.

*SHAPE* cheddar cheese mixture into 8-inch roll. Spread blue cheese mixture evenly over top and sides of roll. Cover with pistachio nuts. Refrigerate several hours. Serve with crackers.

*Makes 10 to 12 servings*

**Tip:** To shape, place cheddar cheese mixture on sheet of plastic wrap; form into roll. Frost with blue cheese mixture. Sprinkle with nuts, securing to top and sides of roll by pressing in with plastic wrap.

# Black Bean Spirals

*Prep time: 15 minutes plus refrigerating*

**1 pkg. (8 oz.) PHILADELPHIA BRAND Cream
  Cheese, softened**
**1 cup (4 oz.) KRAFT Natural Shredded
  Monterey Jack Cheese with Jalapeño
  Peppers***
**½ cup BREAKSTONE'S *or* KNUDSEN Sour
  Cream**
**¼ tsp. onion salt**
**1 cup canned black beans, rinsed, drained**
**3 flour tortillas (10 in.)**
  **Salsa**

*MIX* cheeses, sour cream and onion salt with electric mixer on
medium speed until well blended.

*PLACE* beans in blender or food processor container fitted with
steel blade; cover. Blend until smooth. Spread thin layer of beans on
each tortilla; spread cheese mixture over beans.

*ROLL* tortillas up tightly. Refrigerate 30 minutes. Cut into ½-inch
slices. Serve with salsa. Garnish, if desired.      *Makes 10 servings*

*May also use KRAFT Natural Shredded Monterey Jack Cheese.

**Black Bean Spirals**

# Party Cheese Wreath

*Prep time: 15 minutes plus refrigerating*

> **2 pkg. (8 oz. each) PHILADELPHIA BRAND**
>    **Cream Cheese, softened**
> **1 pkg. (8 oz.) KRAFT Natural Shredded Sharp**
>    **Cheddar Cheese**
> **1 Tbsp. chopped red bell pepper**
> **1 Tbsp. finely chopped onion**
> **2 tsp. Worcestershire sauce**
> **1 tsp. lemon juice**
>    **Dash ground red pepper**
> **¼ cup chopped parsley**
>    **Red and orange bell pepper cutouts**

*MIX* cream cheese and cheddar cheese with electric mixer on medium speed until well blended.

*BLEND* in remaining ingredients except parsley and bell pepper cutouts. Refrigerate several hours or overnight.

*PLACE* drinking glass in center of serving platter. Drop round tablespoonfuls of mixture around glass, just touching outer edge of glass to form ring; smooth with spatula. Remove glass. Garnish with parsley and bell pepper cutouts. Serve with crackers. Garnish, if desired.                                              *Makes 12 servings*

**Mini Cheeseballs:** Shape cream cheese mixture into 1-inch balls. Roll in light rye bread crumbs or dark pumpernickel bread crumbs.

# Corned Beef & Swiss Appetizers

*Prep time: 20 minutes    Broiling time: 3 minutes*

**1 pkg. (8 oz.) PHILADELPHIA BRAND Cream
    Cheese, softened**
**2 tsp. Dijon mustard**
**¼ lb. corned beef, chopped**
**½ cup (2 oz.) KRAFT Natural Shredded Swiss
    Cheese**
**2 Tbsp. chopped green onion**
**36 slices cocktail rye bread, toasted**

**MIX** cream cheese and mustard with electric mixer on medium speed until smooth.

**BLEND** in meat, Swiss cheese and onion. Spread on toast slices. Place on cookie sheet.

**BROIL** 2 to 3 minutes or until lightly browned.

*Makes 3 dozen*

**To Make Ahead:** Prepare as directed except for broiling. Place on cookie sheet. Freeze 1 hour or until firm. Place in freezer-safe zipper-style plastic bags. Freeze up to 1 month. When ready to serve, thaw 10 minutes. Broil as directed.

*Corned Beef & Swiss Appetizers*

## Chicken in Cream Sauce

**Prep time:** *20 minutes*    **Cooking time:** *20 minutes*

**4 boneless skinless chicken breast halves
   (about 1¼ lb.), cut into strips
1 medium red pepper, cut into strips
¼ cup sliced green onions
1 tsp. Italian seasoning
½ tsp. salt
2 Tbsp. butter *or* margarine
¼ cup dry white wine, divided
1 pkg. (8 oz.) PHILADELPHIA BRAND Cream
   Cheese, cubed
½ cup milk
8 oz. linguine, cooked, drained**

*COOK* chicken, vegetables and seasonings in butter in medium skillet on medium heat 10 minutes or until chicken is cooked through, stirring occasionally. Add 2 Tbsp. of the wine; simmer 5 minutes.

*STIR* cream cheese, milk and remaining 2 Tbsp. wine in small saucepan on low heat until smooth.

*PLACE* hot linguine on serving platter; top with chicken mixture and cream cheese mixture. Garnish, if desired.

*Makes 4 to 6 servings*

*Chicken in Cream Sauce*

# Seafood Quiche

*Prep time:* 15 minutes    *Baking time:* 40 minutes plus standing

> **1 pkg. (8 oz.) PHILADELPHIA BRAND Cream
>     Cheese, softened**
> **1 can (6 oz.) crabmeat, drained, flaked**
> **4 eggs**
> **½ cup milk**
> **½ cup sliced green onions**
> **½ tsp. dill weed**
> **½ tsp. lemon and pepper seasoning salt**
> **1 baked pastry shell (9 in.)**

*MIX* all ingredients except pastry shell with electric mixer on medium speed until well blended.

*POUR* into pastry shell.

*BAKE* at 350°F for 40 minutes or until knife inserted in center comes out clean. Let stand 10 minutes before serving. Garnish, if desired.                              *Makes 6 to 8 servings*

*For a luncheon or light dinner, serve with fresh-cut melon slices.*

*Seafood Quiche*

# Twice-Baked Potatoes

*Prep time: 10 minutes plus baking potatoes*    *Baking time: 25 minutes*

**4 large baking potatoes, baked**
**1 pkg. (8 oz.) PHILADELPHIA BRAND Cream**
**Cheese, softened**
**⅓ cup milk**
**½ tsp. salt**
**Dash pepper**
**¼ cup chopped green onions**
**4 slices OSCAR MAYER Bacon, crisply cooked,**
**crumbled**

*CUT* potatoes in half lengthwise; scoop out centers, leaving ⅛-inch shell.

*MASH* potatoes and cream cheese. Add milk and seasonings; beat until fluffy. Stir in onions; spoon into shells. Place on cookie sheet. Top with bacon.

*BAKE* at 350°F for 20 to 25 minutes or until thoroughly heated.

*Makes 8 servings*

*The perfect accompaniment to grilled meats and fresh vegetables.*

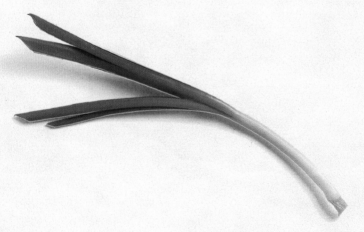

***Twice-Baked Potato***

# Tortellini with Salmon & Dill

**Prep time:** *20 minutes*    **Cooking time:** *10 minutes*

**1 pkg. (8 oz.) PHILADELPHIA BRAND Cream
   Cheese, cubed
⅓ cup milk
½ cup chopped cucumber
3 oz. smoked salmon, cut into thin strips
2 tsp. chopped fresh dill *or* ½ tsp. dill weed
1 pkg. (9 oz.) DI GIORNO Cheese Tortellini,
   cooked, drained**

*STIR* cream cheese and milk in medium saucepan on low heat until smooth. Add cucumber, salmon and dill; heat thoroughly.

*TOSS* with hot tortellini. Garnish, if desired.     *Makes 4 servings*

# Easy Fettuccine Alfredo

**Prep time:** *5 minutes*    **Cooking time:** *15 minutes*

**1 pkg. (8 oz.) PHILADELPHIA BRAND Cream
   Cheese, cubed
1 cup (4 oz.) KRAFT Shredded Parmesan
   Cheese
½ cup (1 stick) butter or margarine
½ cup milk
8 oz. fettuccine, cooked, drained**

*STIR* cream cheese, Parmesan cheese, butter and milk in large saucepan on low heat until smooth.

*ADD* fettuccine; toss lightly. Serve with additional Parmesan cheese, if desired.     *Makes 4 servings*

*Pair this in-a-minute fettuccine alfredo with a Caesar salad.*

**Tortellini with Salmon & Dill**

## Chicken Tetrazzini

**Prep time:** *20 minutes*    **Baking time:** *30 minutes*

½ cup chopped onion
½ cup chopped celery
¼ cup (½ stick) butter or margarine
1 can (13¾ oz.) chicken broth
1 pkg. (8 oz.) PHILADELPHIA BRAND Cream
    Cheese, cubed
¾ cup (3 oz.) KRAFT 100% Grated Parmesan
    Cheese, divided
1 pkg. (7 oz.) spaghetti, cooked, drained
1 jar (6 oz.) whole mushrooms, drained
1 cup chopped cooked chicken or turkey

*COOK* and stir onion and celery in butter in large skillet on medium heat until tender. Add broth, cream cheese and ½ cup of the Parmesan cheese; stir on low heat until cream cheese is melted.

*ADD* remaining ingredients except remaining ¼ cup Parmesan cheese; toss lightly. Spoon into 12×8-inch baking dish; sprinkle with remaining Parmesan cheese.

*BAKE* at 350°F for 30 minutes.                    *Makes 6 servings*

## PHILLY® Mashed Potatoes

**Prep time:** *10 minutes*    **Cooking time:** *30 minutes*

6 cups (2 lbs.) quartered peeled potatoes
½ cup milk
1 pkg. (8 oz.) PHILADELPHIA BRAND Cream
    Cheese, softened
½ tsp. onion powder
½ to ¾ tsp. salt
¼ tsp. pepper
    Paprika

*PLACE* potatoes and enough water to cover in 3-quart saucepan. Bring to a boil. Reduce heat to medium; cook 20 to 25 minutes or until tender. Drain.

*MASH* potatoes, gradually stirring in milk, cream cheese, onion powder, salt and pepper until light and fluffy. Sprinkle with paprika. Serve immediately. *Makes 8 servings*

**To Make Ahead:** Prepare as directed. Spoon into 1½-quart casserole; cover. Refrigerate overnight. When ready to serve, bake, uncovered, at 350°F for 1 hour or until thoroughly heated.

# Creamed Spinach Casserole

*Prep time: 10 minutes    Baking time: 30 minutes*

**2 pkg. (10 oz. each) frozen chopped spinach,
    thawed, well drained
2 pkg. (8 oz. each) PHILADELPHIA BRAND
    Cream Cheese, softened
¼ cup milk
1 tsp. lemon and pepper seasoning salt
⅓ cup crushed seasoned croutons**

*MIX* spinach, cream cheese, milk and seasoning salt until well blended.

*SPOON* mixture into 1-quart casserole. Sprinkle with crushed croutons.

*BAKE* at 350°F for 25 to 30 minutes or until thoroughly heated.
*Makes 6 to 8 servings*

*Perfect for those holiday dinners.*

# Chicken Enchiladas

*Prep time: 20 minutes*    *Baking time: 20 minutes*

**2 cups chopped cooked chicken or turkey**
**1 cup chopped green pepper**
**1 pkg. (8 oz.) PHILADELPHIA BRAND Cream**
    **Cheese, cubed**
**1 jar (8 oz.) salsa, divided**
**6 flour tortillas (6 in.)**
**¾ lb. (12 oz.) VELVEETA Pasteurized Process**
    **Cheese Spread, cut up**
**¼ cup milk**

*STIR* chicken, green pepper, cream cheese and ½ cup of the salsa in medium saucepan on low heat until cream cheese is melted.

*SPOON* approximately ½ cup of the chicken mixture down center of each tortilla; roll up. Place in lightly greased 12×8-inch baking dish.

*STIR* process cheese spread and milk in small saucepan on low heat until smooth. Pour sauce over tortillas; cover with foil.

*BAKE* at 350°F for 20 minutes or until thoroughly heated. Top with remaining salsa. Garnish, if desired.    *Makes 4 to 6 servings*

*Chicken Enchiladas*

*Luscious Desserts*

## Chocolate-Chocolate Cake

*Prep time:* 10 minutes plus cooling    *Baking time:* 1 hour 5 minutes

> **1 pkg. (8 oz.) PHILADELPHIA BRAND Cream Cheese, softened**
> **1 cup BREAKSTONE'S *or* KNUDSEN Sour Cream**
> **½ cup coffee-flavored liqueur *or* water**
> **2 eggs**
> **1 pkg. (2-layer size) chocolate cake mix**
> **1 pkg. (4-serving size) JELL-O Chocolate Flavor Instant Pudding and Pie Filling**
> **1 cup BAKER'S Semi-Sweet Real Chocolate Chips**

*MIX* cream cheese, sour cream, liqueur and eggs with electric mixer on medium speed until well blended. Add cake mix and pudding mix; beat until well blended. Fold in chips. (Batter will be stiff.)

*POUR* into greased and floured 12-cup fluted tube pan.

*BAKE* at 325°F for 1 hour to 1 hour and 5 minutes or until toothpick inserted near center comes out clean. Cool 5 minutes. Remove from pan. Cool completely on wire rack. Sprinkle with powdered sugar before serving. Garnish, if desired.

*Makes 10 to 12 servings*

*Chocolate-Chocolate Cake*

# Cherry Cheesecake Squares

*Prep time: 20 minutes plus refrigerating*    *Baking time: 35 minutes*

**2 cups graham cracker crumbs**
**1 cup sugar, divided**
**¼ cup (½ stick) butter or margarine, melted**
**3 pkg. (8 oz. each) PHILADELPHIA BRAND**
  **Cream Cheese, softened**
**1 tsp. vanilla**
**2 eggs**
**1 can (20 oz.) cherry pie filling**

*MIX* crumbs, ¼ cup of the sugar and butter. Press into 13×9-inch baking pan. Bake at 325°F for 10 minutes.

*MIX* cream cheese, remaining ¾ cup sugar and vanilla with electric mixer on medium speed until well blended. Add eggs; mix just until blended. Pour over crust.

*BAKE* at 325°F for 35 minutes or until center is almost set. Cool. Refrigerate 3 hours or overnight. Top with pie filling. Cut into squares. Garnish, if desired.               *Makes 18 servings*

*Cherry Cheesecake Squares*

# Chilled Lemon Pie

*Prep time: 20 minutes plus refrigerating*

   1 envelope unflavored gelatin
   ¼ cup lemon juice
   2 pkg. (8 oz. each) PHILADELPHIA BRAND
      Cream Cheese, softened
   ½ cup sugar
   1 container (8 oz.) lemon yogurt
   ½ tsp. grated lemon peel
   1 cup whipping cream, whipped
   1 baked pastry shell (9 in.)
      Currant Raspberry Sauce (recipe follows)

*SPRINKLE* gelatin over juice in small saucepan. Let stand
5 minutes to soften. Cook and stir on low heat until gelatin is
completely dissolved. Do not boil.

*MIX* cream cheese and sugar with electric mixer on medium speed
until well blended. Blend in yogurt and peel. Stir in gelatin.
Refrigerate until mixture is slightly thickened but not set.

*FOLD* in whipped cream. Spoon into crust. Refrigerate several
hours or overnight until firm. Serve with Currant Raspberry Sauce.
Garnish, if desired.                    *Makes 8 to 10 servings*

# Currant Raspberry Sauce

   1 pkg. (10 oz.) frozen red raspberries, thawed
   ½ cup KRAFT Red Currant Jelly
   4 tsp. cornstarch

*PLACE* raspberries and jelly in blender or food processor fitted
with steel blade; cover. Process until well blended. Strain.

*STIR* cornstarch and raspberry mixture in small saucepan until
smooth. Bring to boil on medium heat, stirring constantly. Cook
until thickened, stirring constantly. Cool.

*Chilled Lemon Pie*

# Chocolate Truffles

*Prep time: 20 minutes plus refrigerating*

**3 cups sifted powdered sugar**
**1 pkg. (8 oz.) PHILADELPHIA BRAND Cream**
    **Cheese, softened**
**1 pkg. (12 oz.) BAKER'S Semi-Sweet Real**
    **Chocolate Chips, melted**
**1 Tbsp. coffee-flavored liqueur**
**1 Tbsp. orange-flavored liqueur**
**1 Tbsp. almond-flavored liqueur**
    **Ground nuts**
    **Powdered sugar**
    **Unsweetened cocoa**

*ADD* 3 cups powdered sugar gradually to cream cheese, beating with electric mixer on medium speed until well blended. Add melted chocolate; mix well.

*DIVIDE* mixture into thirds. Add different flavored liqueur to each third; mix well. Refrigerate several hours.

*SHAPE* mixtures into 1-inch balls. Roll in nuts, sugar or cocoa. Refrigerate.                    *Makes 5 dozen truffles*

**Microwave Tip:** Place chips in medium microwavable bowl. Microwave on HIGH 1 to 2 minutes or until chips begins to melt, stirring every minute. Remove from oven. Stir until completely melted.

*Chocolate Truffles, Chocolate Fudge*
*(page 58) and White Chocolate*
*Fudge (page 59)*

# Chocolate Fudge

*Prep time: 15 minutes plus refrigerating*

**4 cups sifted powdered sugar**
**1 pkg. (8 oz.) PHILADELPHIA BRAND Cream**
   **Cheese, softened**
**4 squares BAKER'S Unsweetened Chocolate,**
   **melted**
**½ cup chopped nuts**
**1 tsp. vanilla**

***ADD*** sugar gradually to cream cheese, beating with electric mixer on medium speed until well blended. Add remaining ingredients; mix well.

***SPREAD*** into greased 8-inch square pan. Refrigerate several hours.

***CUT*** into 1-inch squares.       *Makes 64 squares*

**Peppermint Fudge:** *Omit nuts and vanilla. Add few drops peppermint extract and ¼ cup crushed peppermint candies. Sprinkle with additional ¼ cup crushed peppermint candies before refrigerating.*

**Cherry Fudge:** *Omit nuts. Add ½ cup chopped maraschino cherries, drained. Garnish with whole maraschino cherries.*

# *White Chocolate Fudge*

*Prep time: 15 minutes plus refrigerating*

**4 cups sifted powdered sugar**
**1 pkg. (8 oz.) PHILADELPHIA BRAND Cream Cheese, softened**
**2 pkg. (6 oz. each) BAKER'S Premium White Chocolate Baking Squares, melted**
**¾ cup chopped dried apricots**
**¾ cup chopped macadamia nuts**
**1½ tsp. vanilla**

*ADD* sugar gradually to cream cheese, beating with electric mixer on medium speed until well blended. Add remaining ingredients; mix well.

*SPREAD* into greased 8-inch square pan. Refrigerate several hours.

*CUT* into 1-inch squares.                               *Makes 64 squares*

# *PHILLY® Frosting*

*Prep time: 10 minutes*

**1 pkg. (8 oz.) PHILADELPHIA BRAND Cream Cheese, softened**
**¼ cup (½ stick) butter or margarine**
**1 tsp. vanilla**
**4 to 4½ cups (approx. 1 lb.) sifted powdered sugar**

*MIX* cream cheese, butter and vanilla with electric mixer on medium speed until well blended.

*ADD* sugar gradually, beating well after each addition.
*Makes enough to fill and frost 2 (8- or 9-inch) cake layers*

**Chocolate PHILLY® Frosting:** *Blend in 3 squares BAKER'S Unsweetened Chocolate, melted.*

# Apple Cranberry Pie

*Prep time: 15 minutes   Baking time: 45 minutes*

**1 pkg. (8 oz.) PHILADELPHIA BRAND Cream
    Cheese, softened**
**½ cup firmly packed brown sugar, divided**
**1 egg**
**1 unbaked pastry shell (9 in.)**
**2 cups sliced peeled apples**
**½ cup halved cranberries**
**1 tsp. ground cinnamon, divided**
**⅓ cup flour**
**⅓ cup old-fashioned or quick-cooking oats,
    uncooked**
**¼ cup (½ stick) butter or margarine**
**¼ cup chopped nuts**

*MIX* cream cheese and ¼ cup of the sugar with electric mixer on medium speed until well blended. Blend in egg. Pour into pastry shell.

*TOSS* apples, cranberries and ½ tsp. of the cinnamon. Spoon over cream cheese mixture.

*MIX* flour, oats, remaining ¼ cup sugar and ½ tsp. cinnamon; cut in butter until mixture resembles coarse crumbs. Stir in nuts. Spoon over fruit mixture.

*BAKE* at 375°F for 40 to 45 minutes or until lightly browned. Cool slightly before serving.                    *Makes 8 to 10 servings*

*Apple Cranberry Pie*

# Flan

*Prep time: 30 minutes plus refrigerating*
*Baking time: 1 hour 20 minutes*

2 cups sugar, divided
½ cup water
1 pkg. (8 oz.) PHILADELPHIA BRAND Cream
    Cheese, softened
1 can (13 oz.) evaporated milk
4 eggs
1 tsp. vanilla
    Dash salt

*STIR* 1 cup of the sugar and water in heavy saucepan on medium-high heat. Boil until syrup turns deep golden brown. Remove from heat; immediately pour into 8- or 9-inch round cake pan, tilting pan to distribute syrup evenly on bottom.

*MIX* cream cheese and remaining 1 cup sugar with electric mixer on medium speed until well blended. Gradually add milk. Blend in eggs, vanilla and salt. Pour over syrup in pan.

*PLACE* pan in large baking pan; place in oven. Pour boiling water into larger pan to about ¾ of the way up sides of cake pan.

*BAKE* at 350°F for 1 hour and 20 minutes or until knife inserted near center comes out clean. Remove cake pan from water; cool. Cover. Refrigerate several hours. To serve, run metal spatula around edge of pan. Unmold onto serving plate. Garnish, if desired.

*Makes 8 to 10 servings*

*Flan*

# PHILLY® Marble Brownies

**Prep time:** *20 minutes plus cooling*   **Baking time:** *40 minutes*

> **1 pkg. (21½ oz.) brownie mix**
> **1 pkg. (8 oz.) PHILADELPHIA BRAND Cream**
> **Cheese, softened**
> **⅓ cup sugar**
> **½ tsp. vanilla**
> **1 egg**
> **1 cup BAKER'S Semi-Sweet Real Chocolate**
> **Chips**

*PREPARE* brownie mix as directed on package. Spread batter in greased 13×9-inch baking pan.

*MIX* cream cheese, sugar and vanilla with electric mixer on medium speed until well blended. Add egg; mix well. Pour over brownie batter; cut through batter with knife several times for marble effect. Sprinkle with chips.

*BAKE* at 350°F for 35 to 40 minutes or until cream cheese mixture is lightly browned. Cool in pan on wire rack. Cut into squares.

*Makes 2 dozen*

# Cranberry Cream Cheese Mold

*Prep time: 30 minutes plus refrigerating*

---

1½ cups boiling water
  1 pkg. (8-serving size) JELL-O Brand
     Cranberry Flavor Gelatin Dessert or any
     red flavor
1½ cups cold water
  ½ tsp. ground cinnamon
  1 medium apple, chopped
  1 cup whole berry cranberry sauce (optional)
  1 pkg. (8 oz.) PHILADELPHIA BRAND Cream
     Cheese, softened

*STIR* boiling water into gelatin in large bowl 2 minutes or until completely dissolved. Stir in cold water and cinnamon.

*POUR* 2 cups of the gelatin into medium bowl. Refrigerate about 1½ hours or until thickened but not set. Reserve remaining 1 cup gelatin at room temperature.

*STIR* apple and cranberry sauce into thickened gelatin. Spoon into 6-cup mold. Refrigerate about 30 minutes or until set but not firm.

*STIR* reserved 1 cup gelatin gradually into cream cheese in small bowl with wire whisk until smooth. Pour over gelatin layer in mold.

*REFRIGERATE* 4 hours or until firm. Unmold. Garnish as desired. Store leftover gelatin mold in refrigerator.

*Makes about 6 cups or 12 servings*

**Unmolding:** Dip mold in hot water for about 15 seconds. Gently pull gelatin from around edges. Place moistened serving plate on top of mold. Invert mold and plate; holding mold and plate together, shake slightly to loosen. Gently remove mold and center gelatin on plate.

# *Magic Dip*

*Prep time: 5 minutes    Microwave time: 4 minutes*

**1 pkg. (8 oz.) PHILADELPHIA BRAND Cream
   Cheese, softened**
**1 cup BAKER'S Semi-Sweet Real Chocolate
   Chips**
**½ cup BAKER'S ANGEL FLAKE Coconut,
   toasted**
**½ cup chopped peanuts**

**SPREAD** cream cheese on bottom of 9-inch microwavable pie
plate or quiche dish.

**TOP** with remaining ingredients.

**MICROWAVE** on MEDIUM (50%) 3 to 4 minutes or until
warm. Serve with graham crackers. Garnish, if desired.

*Makes 6 to 8 servings*

*Perfect for kids.*

*Magic Dip*

# *Praline Bars*

*Prep time:* 30 minutes    *Baking time:* 30 minutes

¾ cup (1½ sticks) butter or margarine,
    softened
1 cup sugar, divided
1 tsp. vanilla, divided
1½ cups flour
2 pkg. (8 oz. each) PHILADELPHIA BRAND
    Cream Cheese, softened
2 eggs
½ cup almond brickle chips
3 Tbsp. caramel ice cream topping

*MIX* butter, ½ cup of the sugar and ½ tsp. of the vanilla with
electric mixer on medium speed until light and fluffy. Gradually add
flour, mixing on low speed until blended. Press onto bottom of
13×9-inch baking pan. Bake at 350°F for 20 to 23 minutes or until
lightly browned.

*MIX* cream cheese, remaining ½ cup sugar and ½ tsp. vanilla with
electric mixer on medium speed until well blended. Add eggs; mix
well. Blend in chips. Pour over crust. Dot top of cream cheese
mixture with topping. Cut through batter with knife several times
for marble effect.

*BAKE* at 350°F for 30 minutes. Cool in pan on wire rack.
Refrigerate. Cut into bars.                        *Makes 2 dozen*

# Peanut-Butter-Banana Brownie Pizza

**Prep time:** 15 minutes    **Baking time:** 20 minutes

 1 pkg. (21½ oz.) brownie mix
 1 pkg. (8 oz.) PHILADELPHIA BRAND Cream
  Cheese, softened
 ¼ cup sugar
 ¼ cup creamy peanut butter
 3 large bananas, peeled, sliced
 ¼ cup coarsely chopped peanuts
 2 squares BAKER'S Semi-Sweet Chocolate
 2 tsp. butter or margarine

*PREPARE* brownie mix as directed on package. Spread batter evenly in greased 12-inch pizza pan. Bake 20 minutes. Cool completely on wire rack.

*MIX* cream cheese, sugar and peanut butter with electric mixer on medium speed until well blended. Spread over brownie. Arrange banana slices over cream cheese mixture; sprinkle with peanuts.

*COOK* chocolate and butter in heavy saucepan on very low heat, stirring constantly until just melted. Drizzle over bananas and peanuts.                                    *Makes 12 servings*

*Peanut-Butter-Banana*
*Brownie Pizza*

# *Irresistible Cheesecakes*

## PHILLY 3-STEP™ *Black Forest Cherry Cheesecake*

*Prep time: 10 minutes    Baking time: 40 minutes*

> 2 pkg. (8 oz. each) PHILADELPHIA BRAND
>    Cream Cheese, softened
> ½ cup sugar
> ½ tsp. vanilla
> 2 eggs
> 4 squares BAKER'S Semi-Sweet Chocolate,
>    melted, slightly cooled
> 1 KEEBLER READY CRUST Chocolate Flavored
>    Pie Crust (6 oz. *or* 9 in.)
> 1 cup thawed COOL WHIP Whipped Topping
> 1½ cups cherry pie filling
> 1 to 2 Tbsp. cherry-flavored liqueur

**1.** **MIX** cream cheese, sugar and vanilla with electric mixer on medium speed until well blended. Add eggs; mix until blended. Blend in melted chocolate.

**2.** **POUR** into crust.

**3.** **BAKE** at 350°F for 40 minutes or until center is almost set. Cool. Refrigerate 3 hours or overnight. Top chilled cheesecake with whipped topping. Mix pie filling and liqueur; spoon over whipped topping. Garnish, if desired.          *Makes 8 servings*

*PHILLY 3-STEP™ Black Forest Cherry Cheesecake*

# PHILLY 3-STEP™ Chocolate Swirl Cheesecake

*Prep time:* 10 minutes    *Baking time:* 40 minutes

**2 pkg. (8 oz. each) PHILADELPHIA BRAND
  Cream Cheese, softened**
**½ cup sugar**
**½ tsp. vanilla**
**2 eggs**
**1 square BAKER'S Unsweetened Chocolate,
  melted, slightly cooled**
**1 KEEBLER READY CRUST Chocolate Flavor
  Pie Crust (6 oz. *or* 9 in.)**

*1. MIX* cream cheese, sugar and vanilla with electric mixer on medium speed until well blended. Add eggs; mix until blended. Blend melted chocolate into ½ cup of the cream cheese batter.

*2. POUR* remaining cream cheese batter into crust. Spoon chocolate batter over cream cheese batter. Cut through batters with knife several times for marble effect.

*3. BAKE* at 350°F for 40 minutes or until center is almost set. Cool. Refrigerate 3 hours or overnight.    *Makes 8 servings*

# PHILLY 3-STEP™ Double Layer Pumpkin Cheesecake

*Prep time: 10 minutes    Baking time: 40 minutes*

2 pkg. (8 oz. each) PHILADELPHIA BRAND
  Cream Cheese, softened
½ cup sugar
½ tsp. vanilla
2 eggs
½ cup canned pumpkin
½ tsp. ground cinnamon
  Dash *each* ground cloves and nutmeg
1 KEEBLER READY CRUST Graham Cracker
  Pie Crust (6 oz. or 9 in.)

**1. MIX** cream cheese, sugar and vanilla with electric mixer on medium speed until well blended. Add eggs; mix until blended. In separate bowl, mix pumpkin and spices. Stir 1 cup of the cream cheese batter into pumpkin mixture.

**2. POUR** remaining cream cheese batter into crust. Top with pumpkin batter.

**3. BAKE** at 350°F for 40 minutes or until center is almost set. Cool. Refrigerate 3 hours or overnight. Garnish, if desired.

*Makes 8 servings*

**PHILLY 3-STEP™ Double Layer
Pumpkin Cheesecake**

# PHILLY 3-STEP™ Fruit Topped Cheesecake

*Prep time: 10 minutes    Cooking time: 40 minutes*

**2 pkg. (8 oz. each) PHILADELPHIA BRAND
   Cream Cheese, softened
½ cup sugar
½ tsp. vanilla
2 eggs
1 KEEBLER READY CRUST Graham Cracker
   Crumb Pie Crust (6 oz. or 9 in.)
2 cups fresh fruit slices
2 Tbsp. KRAFT Strawberry or Apple Jelly,
   heated (optional)**

1. *MIX* cream cheese, sugar and vanilla with electric mixer on medium speed until well blended. Add eggs; mix until blended.

2. *POUR* into crust.

3. *BAKE* at 350°F for 40 minutes or until center is almost set. Cool. Refrigerate 3 hours or overnight. Top with fruit; drizzle with jelly, if desired.                    *Makes 8 servings*

*PHILLY 3-STEP™ Fruit Topped Cheesecake*

# *Cappuccino Cheesecake*

*Prep time: 25 minutes plus refrigerating*   **Baking time:** *1 hour*

> **1 cup chocolate wafer cookie crumbs**
> **3 Tbsp. sugar**
> **3 Tbsp. butter or margarine, melted**
> **4 pkg. (8 oz. each) PHILADELPHIA BRAND**
> **    Cream Cheese, softened**
> **1 cup sugar**
> **2 Tbsp. flour**
> **2 tsp. vanilla**
> **4 eggs**
> **1 Tbsp. MAXWELL HOUSE Instant Coffee**
> **3 Tbsp. coffee-flavored liqueur**

**MIX** crumbs, 3 Tbsp. sugar and butter; press onto bottom and 2 inches up sides of 9-inch springform pan. Bake at 325°F for 10 minutes.

**MIX** cream cheese, 1 cup sugar, flour and vanilla with electric mixer on medium speed until well blended. Add eggs, 1 at a time, mixing on low speed after each addition, just until blended. Stir instant coffee into liqueur until dissolved. Blend into batter. Pour into crust.

**BAKE** at 325°F for 55 minutes to 1 hour or until center is almost set. Run knife or metal spatula around rim of pan to loosen cake; cool before removing rim of pan. Refrigerate 4 hours or overnight. Garnish with chocolate-dipped almonds or chocolate-covered coffee beans. *Makes 12 servings*

# Brownie Bottom Cheesecake

*Prep time: 40 minutes plus refrigerating*    *Baking time: 1 hour*

½ cup (1 stick) butter or margarine
4 squares BAKER'S Unsweetened Chocolate
2¼ cups sugar, divided
2 eggs
¼ cup milk
2 tsp. vanilla, divided
1 cup flour
½ tsp. salt
3 pkg. (8 oz. each) PHILADELPHIA BRAND
    Cream Cheese, softened
3 eggs
½ cup BREAKSTONE'S or KNUDSEN Sour
    Cream

*MELT* butter and chocolate in 3-quart heavy saucepan on very low heat, stirring constantly; cool. Blend in 1½ cups of the sugar.

*ADD* 2 of the eggs, 1 at a time, mixing on low speed after each addition until blended. Blend in milk and 1 tsp. of the vanilla. Mix flour and salt. Add to chocolate mixture, mixing just until blended. Spread evenly onto bottom of greased and floured 9-inch springform pan. Bake at 325°F for 25 minutes.

*MIX* cream cheese, remaining ¾ cup sugar and 1 tsp. vanilla with electric mixer on medium speed until well blended. Add remaining 3 eggs, 1 at a time, mixing on low speed after each addition just until blended. Blend in sour cream; pour over brownie bottom. (Filling will almost come to top of pan.)

*BAKE* at 325°F for 55 minutes to 1 hour or until center is almost set. Run knife or metal spatula around rim of pan to loosen cake; cool before removing rim of pan. Refrigerate 4 hours or overnight. Let stand at room temperature 30 minutes before serving. Drizzle with assorted ice cream toppings, if desired.          *Makes 12 servings*

# PHILLY 3-STEP™ Mini Cheesecakes

**Prep time:** *10 minutes*     **Baking time:** *20 minutes*

> **2 pkg. (8 oz. each) PHILADELPHIA BRAND
>    Cream Cheese, softened**
> **½ cup sugar**
> **½ tsp. vanilla**
> **2 eggs**
> **2 pkg. (4 oz. each) KEEBLER READY CRUST
>    Single Serve Graham Cracker Pie Crusts
>    (12 crusts)**

**1. MIX** cream cheese, sugar and vanilla with electric mixer on medium speed until well blended. Add eggs; mix until blended.

**2. POUR** into crusts placed on cookie sheet.

**3. BAKE** at 350°F for 20 minutes or until centers are almost set. Cool. Refrigerate 2 hours or overnight. Top with whipped topping or fresh fruit and strawberry glaze, if desired. Garnish, if desired.          *Makes 12 servings*

**PHILLY 3-STEP™ Mini Cheesecakes**

# PHILLY 3-STEP™ White Chocolate Almond Cheesecake

**Prep time:** 10 minutes    **Baking time:** 40 minutes

**2 pkg. (8 oz. each) PHILADELPHIA BRAND Cream Cheese, softened**
**½ cup sugar**
**½ tsp. vanilla**
**2 eggs**
**1 pkg. (6 oz.) BAKER'S Premium White Chocolate Baking Squares, chopped, divided**
**1 KEEBLER READY CRUST Graham Cracker Pie Crust (6 oz. or 9 in.)**
**½ cup chopped almonds**

1. **MIX** cream cheese, sugar and vanilla with electric mixer on medium speed until well blended. Add eggs; mix until blended. Stir in ½ cup of the white chocolate.

2. **POUR** into crust. Sprinkle with almonds and remaining white chocolate.

3. **BAKE** at 350°F for 40 minutes or until center is almost set. Cool. Refrigerate 3 hours or overnight. Garnish, if desired.

*Makes 8 servings*

**PHILLY 3-STEP™ White Chocolate Almond Cheesecake**

# PHILLY 3-STEP™ Tirami Su Cheesecake

**Prep time:** *10 minutes*    **Baking time:** *40 minutes*

     2 pkg. (8 oz. each) PHILADELPHIA BRAND
        Cream Cheese, softened
     ½ cup sugar
     ½ tsp. vanilla
     2 eggs
     2 Tbsp. brandy
    12 ladyfingers, split
     ½ cup strong black coffee
     1 cup thawed COOL WHIP Whipped Topping
     1 square BAKER'S Semi-Sweet Chocolate,
        shaved

**1.** **MIX** cream cheese, sugar and vanilla with electric mixer on medium speed until well blended. Add eggs; mix until blended. Stir in brandy. Arrange ladyfingers on bottom and sides of 9-inch pie plate; drizzle with coffee.

**2.** **POUR** cream cheese mixture into prepared pie plate.

**3.** **BAKE** at 350°F for 40 minutes or until center is almost set. Cool. Refrigerate 3 hours or overnight. Top with whipped topping and shaved chocolate just before serving. Garnish, if desired.                                    *Makes 8 servings*

**PHILLY 3-STEP™ Tirami Su Cheesecake**

# PHILLY 3-STEP™ Caramel Pecan Cheesecake

*Prep time:* 10 minutes    *Baking time:* 40 minutes

**2 pkg. (8 oz. each) PHILADELPHIA BRAND**
  **Cream Cheese, softened**
**½ cup sugar**
**½ tsp. vanilla**
**2 eggs**
**20 caramels**
**2 Tbsp. milk**
**½ cup chopped pecans**
**1 KEEBLER READY CRUST Graham Cracker**
  **Pie Crust (6 oz. or 9 in.)**

**1. MIX** cream cheese, sugar and vanilla with electric mixer on medium speed until well blended. Add eggs; mix until blended. Melt caramels with milk in small saucepan on low heat, stirring frequently until smooth. Stir in pecans.

**2. POUR** caramel mixture into crust. Pour cream cheese batter over caramel mixture.

**3. BAKE** at 350°F for 40 minutes or until center is almost set. Cool. Refrigerate 3 hours or overnight. Garnish, if desired.

*Makes 8 servings*

**Chocolate Caramel Pecan Cheesecake:** *Blend 4 squares BAKER'S Semi-Sweet Chocolate, melted and slightly cooled, into batter. Continue as directed.*

# New York Cheesecake

*Prep time: 15 minutes plus refrigerating*
*Baking time: 1 hour 10 minutes*

**1 cup graham cracker crumbs**
**3 Tbsp. sugar**
**3 Tbsp. butter or margarine, melted**
**5 pkg. (8 oz. each) PHILADELPHIA BRAND**
**   Cream Cheese, softened**
**1 cup sugar**
**3 Tbsp. flour**
**1 Tbsp. vanilla**
**3 eggs**
**1 cup BREAKSTONE'S or KNUDSEN Sour**
**   Cream**

*MIX* crumbs, 3 Tbsp. sugar and butter; press onto bottom of 9-inch springform pan. Bake at 350°F for 10 minutes.

*MIX* cream cheese, 1 cup sugar, flour and vanilla with electric mixer on medium speed until well blended. Add eggs, 1 at a time, mixing on low speed after each addition, just until blended. Blend in sour cream. Pour over crust.

*BAKE* 1 hour and 5 minutes to 1 hour and 10 minutes or until center is almost set. Run knife or metal spatula around rim of pan to loosen cake; cool before removing rim of pan. Refrigerate 4 hours or overnight. Top with cherry pie filling and garnish, if desired.

*Makes 12 servings*

**Chocolate New York Cheesecake:** *Substitute 1 cup chocolate wafer cookie crumbs for graham cracker crumbs. Blend 8 squares BAKER'S Semi-Sweet Chocolate, melted and slightly cooled, into batter. Continue as directed.*

**New York Cheesecake**

# White Chocolate Cheesecake

*Prep time: 35 minutes plus refrigerating*    *Baking time: 1 hour*

- ½ cup (1 stick) butter or margarine
- ¾ cup sugar, divided
- 1½ tsp. vanilla, divided
- 1 cup flour
- 4 pkg. (8 oz. each) PHILADELPHIA BRAND Cream Cheese, softened
- 4 eggs
- 2 pkg. (6 oz. each) BAKER'S Premium White Chocolate Baking Squares, melted, slightly cooled

*MIX* butter, ¼ cup of the sugar and ½ tsp. of the vanilla with electric mixer on medium speed until light and fluffy. Gradually add flour, mixing on low speed until blended. Press onto bottom of 9-inch springform pan; prick with fork. Bake at 325°F for 25 minutes or until edges are light golden brown.

*MIX* cream cheese, remaining ½ cup sugar and 1 tsp. vanilla with electric mixer on medium speed until well blended. Add eggs, 1 at a time, mixing on low speed after each addition just until blended. Blend in melted chocolate. Pour over crust.

*BAKE* at 325°F for 55 minutes to 1 hour or until center is almost set. Run knife or metal spatula around rim of pan to loosen cake; cool before removing rim of pan. Refrigerate 4 hours or overnight. Garnish, if desired.                    *Makes 12 servings*

**White Chocolate Macadamia Nut Cheesecake:** *Stir 1 jar (3½ oz.) macadamia nuts, chopped (about ¾ cup), into batter.*

*White Chocolate Cheesecake*

# METRIC CONVERSION CHART

## VOLUME MEASUREMENTS (dry)

⅛ teaspoon = 0.5 mL

¼ teaspoon = 1 mL

½ teaspoon = 2 mL

¾ teaspoon = 4 mL

1 teaspoon = 5 mL

1 tablespoon = 15 mL

2 tablespoons = 30 mL

¼ cup = 60 mL

⅓ cup = 75 mL

½ cup = 125 mL

⅔ cup = 150 mL

¾ cup = 175 mL

1 cup = 250 mL

2 cups = 1 pint = 500 mL

3 cups = 750 mL

4 cups = 1 quart = 1 L

## VOLUME MEASUREMENTS (fluid)

1 fluid ounce (2 tablespoons) = 30 mL

4 fluid ounces (½ cup) = 125 mL

8 fluid ounces (1 cup) = 250 mL

12 fluid ounces (1½ cups) = 375 mL

16 fluid ounces (2 cups) = 500 mL

## WEIGHTS (mass)

½ ounce = 15 g

1 ounce = 30 g

3 ounces = 90 g

4 ounces = 120 g

8 ounces = 225 g

10 ounces = 285 g

12 ounces = 360 g

16 ounces = 1 pound = 450 g

## DIMENSIONS

1/16 inch = 2 mm

⅛ inch = 3 mm

¼ inch = 6 mm

½ inch = 1.5 cm

¾ inch = 2 cm

1 inch = 2.5 cm

## OVEN TEMPERATURES

250°F = 120°C

275°F = 140°C

300°F = 150°C

325°F = 160°C

350°F = 180°C

375°F = 190°C

400°F = 200°C

425°F = 220°C

450°F = 230°C

## BAKING PAN SIZES

| Utensil | Size in Inches/ Quarts | Metric Volume | Size in Centimeters |
|---|---|---|---|
| Baking or Cake Pan (square or rectangular) | 8×8×2 | 2 L | 20×20×5 |
| | 9×9×2 | 2.5 L | 23×23×5 |
| | 12×8×2 | 3 L | 30×20×5 |
| | 13×9×2 | 3.5 L | 33×23×5 |
| Loaf Pan | 8×4×3 | 1.5 L | 20×10×7 |
| | 9×5×3 | 2 L | 23×13×7 |
| Round Layer Cake Pan | 8×1½ | 1.2 L | 20×4 |
| | 9×1½ | 1.5 L | 23×4 |
| Pie Plate | 8×1¼ | 750 mL | 20×3 |
| | 9×1¼ | 1 L | 23×3 |
| Baking Dish or Casserole | 1 quart | 1 L | — |
| | 1½ quart | 1.5 L | — |
| | 2 quart | 2 L | — |